St. John's

N E W F O U N D L A N D

Nimbus Publishing Ltd.
P.O. Box 9301 Station A
Halifax, Nova Scotia B3K 5N5
(902) 455-4286

Design: Stewart Moss

Printed and bound in Hong Kong by
Everbest Printing Co. Ltd.

Canadian Cataloguing in Publication Data
Hansen, Ben, 1927-
St. John's Newfoundland
     Originally published: Dartmouth, N.S.:
     James-StoneHouse Publications, 1991.
ISBN 1-55109-241-7

1. St. John's (Nfld.) — Pictorial works.   I. Title.
FC2196.37.H36 1998   971.8'104'0222   C98-950023-3
F1124.5.S14H36 1998

Kodachrome film and Nikon cameras were used to
photograph the images.

Photographs of the Commissariat House,
Newfoundland Museum, and Quidi Vidi Battery
courtesy of Minister of Municipal and Provincial Affairs.

St. John's

NEWFOUNDLAND

Photography by
Ben Hansen

Introduction by
Shane O'Dea

Captions by Derek Yetman
Graphic Design by Stewart Moss GDC

NIMBUS
PUBLISHING LTD

Introduction

St. John's is a town that has grown out of the sea—in both senses of the word. It has come from the sea because its being has been based on its harbour and the fishery beyond. But it has also grown up to grow away from the sea, to become a center for commerce and government—activities other than those of the sea. This should not surprise us for what is a port but shelter from the sea and St. John's is a superb port because of its very capacity to afford almost perfect shelter. The Narrows give only the tightest glimpse of the Atlantic and, if you move a short distance up the harbour, that glimpse is gone to be replaced by a solid wall of Southside and Signal Hill.

In that interaction with the sea is St. John's history. The safety of its harbour made it the logical gathering point of the fleets that started prosecuting the fishery in the sixteenth century. It was to this crowded port that Sir Humphrey Gilbert came in the summer of 1583 to claim Newfoundland and the adjacent territories for England. And when the first colony was established in 1610 St. John's was considered *"the principall prime and chief lot in all the whole countrey"*. It had, by virtue of its land and its location, made itself the capital. The land provided safe harbour for vessels; the location was the nearest to Europe. But, in the use of the word "capital" one has to be careful. St. John's was capital of very little in the seventeenth century: a few houses, a number of fishing premises. There was no sense of permanence, no institution, no law. That did not come until the end of the seventeenth century. The building of a fort and a church brought the order necessary to the growth of a real town and enabled it to survive several destructive raids by the French.

At the end of the eighteenth century St. John's began, as did the whole of Newfoundland, to grow phenomenally and was, until about 1820, the port of choice for many of the Irish immigrants. Those immigrants took over the town — its politics, its character, its dialect — and gave it a colour I am sure the establishment felt it could have done without in the nineteenth century. Much of this colour has to do with local politics and much of local politics had a lot to do with the churches. The great towering presence of the Basilica on the hill above the town is a product not of design but of available land. Its builder, Bishop Michael Anthony Fleming, was determined to make a statement about the place and power of the Catholics in the community and his church did that. And as if to emphasize his point, further down the hill, beneath the Basilica stands the Anglican Cathedral of St. John the Baptist, a Gothic Revival masterwork awaiting the construction of its tower and spire to give it its proper place in the town.

The other characteristic feature of Victorian St. John's was fire. Early in the century there were still fish flakes all along the waterfront. They were hazardous enough with their dried timber and drier boughs and went after a series of fires in 1816–17. But seal and cod liver oil were equally flammable and contributed to the destruction of the city in 1846. The last Great Fire was in 1892 and, sweeping down Long's Hill it took the Anglican Cathedral and the whole East End of the city. It was this 1892 Fire that left a major mark on the architecture of the city, both commercial and domestic. All the stores on Water St. had to be rebuilt from Bowrings eastward and they were still there until the 1970s when—as Ben Hansen's photographs show—a tension developed between the old and the new. In the residential areas, on the hill above Water and Duckworth Streets, the older forms survive restored in the Heritage Conservation Area. Those houses with their mansard roofs and bay windows represent the new style that came in after the fire, copying the grander styles of the large merchant houses on Rennie's Mill Road. Much of the old city is architecturally intact —a feature which sets the town apart from many others in North America. But the other surprising survival is the layout of the streets and lanes which follow no orderly gridiron but, rather, reflect the paths made by adults and children and animals in another age when the steepness of the hills determined the way.

Hansen's photographs capture the sense of the town changed and unchanged; of its people and what they have made, of what they are made; of its place from hill to harbour and the sea beyond.

Shane O'Dea
Center for Material Culture Studies
Memorial University of Newfoundland

St. John's harbour at daybreak. The Portuguese explorer Gaspar Corte Real is believed to have arrived
here in the year 1500, giving the name Rio de San Johem, or St. John's River, to a stream flowing into the harbour.

St. John's is the first Canadian city to see the sun. Its arrival heralds the end of another night's vigil for the Fort Amherst lighthouse.

The red glow of morning greets an inshore fishing boat as it leaves the harbour. St. John's has been a centre of the Newfoundland fishery for almost 500 years.

The schooner Scademia sails past Fort Amherst on its first tourist cruise of the day.
The vessel is a familiar sight throughout the summer, delighting visitors and locals alike.

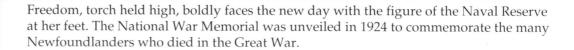

Freedom, torch held high, boldly faces the new day with the figure of the Naval Reserve at her feet. The National War Memorial was unveiled in 1924 to commemorate the many Newfoundlanders who died in the Great War.

Early morning mist lingers on the surface of Georges Pond on Signal Hill.
The pond has been an active and alternate source of water for the city since 1846.

The M/V Sanderling navigates the Narrows leading into St. John's harbour.
The channel has been a test of helmsmen's skills for centuries.

Busy old fool, unruly Sun,
Why dost thou thus,
Through windows, and through curtains call on us?
–John Donne

Kilometer "0" of the Trans Canada Highway outside St. John's City Hall. At this point the highway is still New Gower Street, once known as Middle Street.

The upper end of colourful and historic Victoria Street, against a backdrop of the Narrows.

Scotia Tower, monument to the modern age, stands where codfish once dried in the sun. Fishing boats still berth just yards away.

A busker entertains passers-by with his fiddle outside Atlantic Place on Water Street. Street performers keep the musical traditions of the city in tune throughout the summer.

The LSPU Hall on Victoria Street. Once the meeting hall of the Longshoremen's Protective Union, it is now a major centre for the arts.

The lower end of Victoria Street. Before the neighbourhood was destroyed by one of the great fires of the 1800's, the street was known as Meeting House Lane.

An ice-cream vendor draws customers near the Scotia Tower as the day begins to warm.

The choreographer of downtown traffic, Constable Frank Miller of the Royal Newfoundland Constabulary keeps vehicles moving at the intersection of Prescott and Duckworth Streets.

The architecture of Water Street is a unique blend of styles from various periods, evoking a strong sense of the city's history.

Despite the case for Gaspar Corte Real's discovery of St. John's harbour, tradition has it that John Cabot became the first European to set eyes upon it on the feast day of St. John the Baptist, June 24, 1497.

The modern commercial face of the St. John's harbourfront.

A relic from the days of sail, its original purpose long since served, adorns the lawn of the Battery Hotel.

Brightly painted boats line the harbour apron as their crews prepare for another voyage to the fishing grounds.

The West Tower of the Basilica. Consecrated in 1855, the church is constructed of limestone and granite quarried in Newfoundland and Ireland.

St. John the Baptist looks to sea from the arch of the Basilica which bears his name. The centre of Roman Catholic faith in St. John's, the Basilica dominates the landscape above the harbour.

Solitary footprints lead to the doors of the Anglican Cathedral. The church was consecrated in 1850 and is regarded as one of the finest examples of Gothic architecture in the New World.

In another season the Cathedral steps are warmed by a bride and groom with their wedding party.

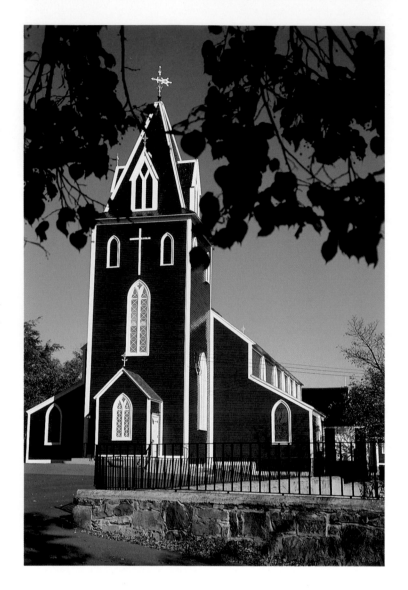

St. Thomas's Anglican Church, opened in 1836,
is also known as the Old Garrison Church.
It once served the soldiers stationed at nearby Fort William.

The Colonial Building was the seat of the
Newfoundland legislature from its opening
in 1850 until 1959. The stately Classical Revival
building now houses the Provincial Archives.

Devon Row, which survived the Great Fire of 1892. Occupants and servants of the four-storey brick and wood houses kept the roof wet with buckets of water and swept sparks away with their brooms.

The Family Court building has taken its proud place among much older neighbours on King's Bridge Road.

The Baine Johnson Centre reflects the clouds and a nearby building in its mirrored walls.

Hotel Newfoundland rises behind the stone houses of Temperance Street.

Tulips splash their colour across the lawn of the building which houses the Newfoundland and Labrador Housing Corporation.

7 Victoria Street and 7 Forest Road, with architectural features as close as their numbers.

Commissariat House, the simple but elegant quarters and offices of the
Assistant Commissary General. Costumed guides await the next group of visitors.

The kitchen of Commissariat House. The Georgian building is restored and decorated to the period of 1830.

A four-poster bed and other furnishings in the principal bedroom of Commissariat House.

Neatly labelled bottles of medicines are
displayed behind the counter of Apothecary Hall.

A "Show Globe" in the window of Apothecary Hall
once identified the nature of the business conducted within.

The restored drugstore dates from circa 1895,
complete with fixtures of oak made in England in 1879.

The Newfoundland Museum, completed in 1907, houses exhibits of the province's 9000 year history.

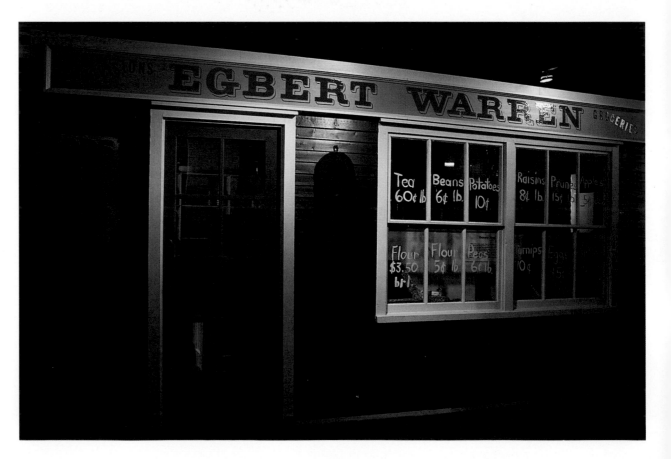

The Working World of Egbert Warren, a Newfoundland Museum exhibit of commercial life in St. John's at the turn of the century.

Lar's Fruit Mart, characteristically resplendent at the corner of New Gower and Queen Streets.

Eye-catching storefronts ensure that shoppers
know where to find what they want.

Mr. Gerald Seaward of the Seaview Grocery, Carter's Hill. If he doesn't have it, you don't need it.

The flags spell Bowrings, a department store which still bears the name of one of the city's early merchant families.

The beautifully restored Murray Premises now houses shops, offices and a museum. In the 19th century it was used for the drying and storing of salted cod.

The Village Mall offers shoppers a central fountain and escalators,
though not the salt air of Water Street.

The fountain at Prince Edward Plaza, situated between Duckworth and George Streets. The old city hall once stood on the site.

Water from the plaza's fountain takes on the colour of the brightly painted buildings next door.

The figures of the Forestry Corps and the Merchant Marine at the base of the National War Memorial.

*S*erene will be our days and bright,
And happy will our nature be,
When love is an unerring light,
And joy its own security.
　　　　　　　　　–William Wordsworth

John Cabot was long thought to have been the first European to arrive at Newfoundland's shores. In fact, Norsemen preceded him by five centuries.

Sir Wilfred Grenfell, the man who devoted his life to establishing medical care facilities in Labrador and Northern Newfoundland.

The plaque commemorating Newfoundland's first radio broadcast in July of 1924. The radio station, now called VOWR, still operates from Wesley United Church.

The city's most famous landmark—Cabot Tower—was built between 1898 and 1900 to commemorate the 400th anniversary of Cabot's discovery and Queen Victoria's Diamond Jubilee.

A fearsome iceberg, calved from an Arctic glacier thousands of miles away,
rests off Fort Amherst before continuing its journey south.

The American sailing ship Society Explorer enters the Narrows
with her sails furled on June 24, St. John's Day. Fort Amherst is in the foreground.

Signal Hill, long a witness to man's wanderings upon the sea,
is pictured with the lights of vessels which now carry us by land and air.

Soldiers fall in behind flag and drum as the Signal Hill Tattoo marches into battle. A Newfoundland dog acts as mascot.

The Tattoo demonstrates a British Square, a defensive formation common in the 19th century.

The measure of an army is the strength of its discipline. Infringements of military regulations were met with harsh punishment.

Crowds thrill to the crackling of musket fire and the boom of cannon.
The harbour provides a magnificent backdrop to the outdoor theatre.

A wall mural portrays the crossroads at the west end of Water Street at the turn of the century, when modern technology began to displace a more traditional mode of transportation. The streetcars of St. John's ran from 1900 until 1948.

Popular issues of the day are depicted in a mural on McBride's Hill which commemorates the centenary of the city's incorporation in 1888.

The entrance to Government House on Military Road, official residence of the province's Lieutenant Governor. The house was constructed between 1827 and 1831.

The weather cooperates at the Lieutenant Governor's annual Garden Party on the lawn of Government House. Hats are an integral part of the tradition.

A brightly hued banner advertises the
Peace A Chord festival in Bannerman Park.

Who could miss that banner? Thousands crowd the park for the
yearly festival of music in aid of world peace.

Bannerman Park has been an oasis in the heart of the city since 1891.
It is named for Governor Alexander Bannerman, who donated land to help create the park.

The pond near Mt. Scio Road which lends its name to the Memorial University Botanical Garden at Oxen Pond. The garden is a 45 hectare area of native flora and fauna, developed for education, research and public enjoyment.

When daisies pied and violets blue,
And lady-smocks all silver white,
And cuckoo-buds of yellow hue
Do paint the meadows with delight.
–William Shakespeare

Herring Gulls await the return of Battery fishermen
and the chance of a mid-day meal.

Startled from their resting place below Gibbet Hill,
a flock of gulls soars over the roofs of the Battery.

The Battery, an outport neighbourhood within the city, has been known by that name since at least 1673, when gun emplacements located there contributed to the city's defence against the Dutch.

Sunshine turns to fog within minutes at the Battery, making the drying of clothes an unpredictable affair.

Their bows pointing into the wind, a quartet of identically painted fishing boats lies at their moorings near the Battery.

With their boats moored and the nets
spread to dry, fishermen take time
for a yarn on a Battery stage.

The familiar summer ritual of preparing the house against another year of Newfoundland weather.

Renovations on Bates Hill, which runs between Queen's Road and the western end of Duckworth Street.

Back yards and streets are converted to outdoor drying facilities on a sunny summer's day.

The small inlet of Quidi Vidi, known locally as the Gut.
Prominent Cuckold's Head separates the Gut from Cuckold's Cove.

Tranquil Quidi Vidi remains a distinct enclave within the city.
Equally enduring are the debates about the origin of the name, as well as its pronunciation.

On a stony cliff above Quidi Vidi, wild roses thrive in spite of the chilly summer fogs.

The Quidi Vidi Battery guards the entrance to the Gut. The small fort and gun emplacement are restored to the period of the War of 1812.

Mallard Cottage in Quidi Vidi, now an antique shop, is one of the city's oldest houses.

Boats and gear are safely out of the water by the time the first freeze comes to Quidi Vidi.

An early winter evening arrives, and a door on New Gower Street projects an image of warmth within.

The Anthony Tooton house on LeMarchant Road, once owned by the man who brought the Kodak camera to St. John's.

Good night to the season! 'Tis over!
Gay dwellings no longer are gay;
The courtier, the gambler, the lover,
Are scattered like swallows away.

—W. M. Praed

St. Bonaventure's College, completed in 1859 to serve as a Roman Catholic seminary. It became a non-clerical school in 1870 and remains so today.

61

St. John's harbour, "caught over" on a frosty winter's day.

Skaters enjoy a perfect day on Kenny's Pond. Every neighbourhood
seems to have a pond nearby for winter fun.

The Caribou, symbol of the Royal Newfoundland Regiment. The statue in Bowring Park is a memorial to the regiment which fought courageously throughout Europe during the Great War—and was virtually annihilated at the Battle of the Somme.

The Waterford River as it flows through Bowring Park. This was the river which Gaspar Corte Real named Rio de San Johem around the year 1500.

Two perspectives on the beauty of Bowring Park.
A silver thaw holds plants and trees in its sparkling grip,
and a few months later crocuses herald the arrival of spring.

The statue of Peter Pan in Bowring Park. The statue was erected by Sir Edgar Bowring in memory of his niece, who drowned in the wreck of the S.S. Florizel.

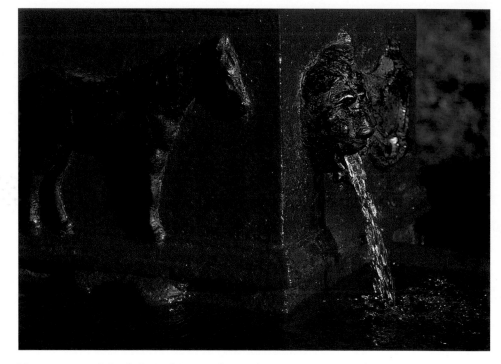

Horses once slaked their thirst at the park's cast iron trough, one of many which were found throughout the city.

The Bowring Park swans, captured in a moment of graceful symmetry.

Neighbours gather for an afternoon chat
in O'Brien Park at the bottom of Signal Hill Road.

Children frolic on a downtown street
during the carefree days of summer.

A group of Patrick Street pals
hams it up for the camera.

The jewel of the city's lakes and ponds, Quidi Vidi Lake attracts windsurfers, sailers, rowers, canoeists and kayakers. The group depends upon the strength of the wind.

Tourists seem unable to resist photographing the carefully restored Queen's Battery overlooking the Narrows or the Quidi Vidi Battery guarding the Gut.

The schooner Scademia under partial sail in the Narrows.
The tour boat leaves Pier 7 four times a day, usually
with a full complement of passengers.

The 26 metre Scademia offers the uninitiated a chance to jig for cod,
watch humpback whales and enjoy a few hours on the water.

Admiral Johns, official host of the St. John's Day celebrations, with two of his crew.

St. John's Day, the municipal holiday when crowds come out to view the Caplin Sex Sorting Contest, the Lobster Races and the Kiss the Cod Lottery.

The Discovery Day Sailing Race, which begins in St. John's harbour and ends at
Long Pond in Conception Bay. Competitors tack for position near the start line.

The George Street Folk Festival on St. John's Day. Prince Edward Plaza becomes
an outdoor theatre for traditional music, song and dance.

A juggler entertains at a family picnic and street performance festival in C.A. Pippy Park, a recreational area of 1343 hectares within the northern boundaries of the city.

Flowers brighten windows and doorways during the warm summer months.

Despite the problem of space, many downtown homeowners are enthusiastic gardeners.

At Fort Amherst parking space may be at a premium, but there's always room on the line for another pair of socks.

*Beneath his ebon nose
Mouth like a small lion shows;
And around his mouth there grew
A small beard of silvery hue.*
—Joachim du Bellay

On Harbour Drive, the glass and chrome of a
tractor trailer and the Scotia Tower.

A highrise from another period,
commanding the heights of Tessier Place.

Isabella St. John practices her craft in her
Blue Moon Pottery studio at the Battery.

Artist Graham Howcroft with one of his stained glass creat
Ubiquitous Signal Hill looms in the background.

The St. John's Arts and Culture Centre, which was opened in 1967. An untitled sculpture by Peter Walker graces the lawn.

North America's oldest continuous sporting event draws thousands to Quidi Vidi Lake on the first Wednesday of August. The annual St. John's Regatta dates from 1826.

Coxswains and oarsmen ready their racing shells for the starting gun. What likely began as a
dory rowing contest among fishermen has evolved into a municipal holiday and a major sporting event.

Entertainment for the kids and games of chance are as much a tradition at the Regatta as the races, which are sometimes forgotten amid the many distractions.

"Round and round she goes. Where she stops nobody knows." Eyes are glued to the spinning wheels in hopes of winning a stuffed bear or other prize.

The beautiful Rennie's River walking trail, which dissects the city from Long Pond to Quidi Vidi. Few cities can boast a clean river, full of trout, running through its centre.

The Shadow Pools at Bowring Park. They were designed by the architects of the park to give a vivid reflection of the trees and waterfowl.

Memorial University of Newfoundland, established in 1925 as a memorial to those who had lost
their lives on active service during the Great War. Originally a college, it gained university status shortly after
Newfoundland's entry into Confederation.

The Newfoundland Freshwater Resource Centre, where visitors can observe the fish, plant and insect life of an outdoor stream from an underwater perspective. This fluvarium is the first of its kind in North America.

The Marine Institute as evening approaches. The college provides training to students pursuing careers in marine technology.

The 90 metre Ice Tank at the Institute for Marine Dynamics is the largest in the world.
The tank is used for research on the design of icebreakers and structures which operate in ice.

A computerized milling machine reproduces a sailboat design at the Institute for Marine Dynamics.

A scale model of an offshore drilling structure is tested in the Ocean Engineering Basin at the Institute for Marine Dynamics.

A tugboat quickly traverses the 2 km length of the harbour. St. John's has been called
one of the finest natural harbours in the world because of the shelter it provides.

Fishing boats are safely berthed as a fog bank extends a long arm into the harbour.
Even on a brilliant summer day the fog can creep quietly through the Narrows.

The Sir Wilfred Grenfell, a Canadian Coast Guard rescue tug, heads for the open sea.

When Sir Humphrey Gilbert arrived at St. John's in 1583 to claim Newfoundland for the English crown, he was surprised upon entering the harbour, "there being within of all nations to the number of 36 sail." The harbour is still an international port of call.

The influence of the sea and the romantic allure of sailing ships
is evident in the models proudly displayed in downtown windows. . .

. . .and in more than a few backyards.

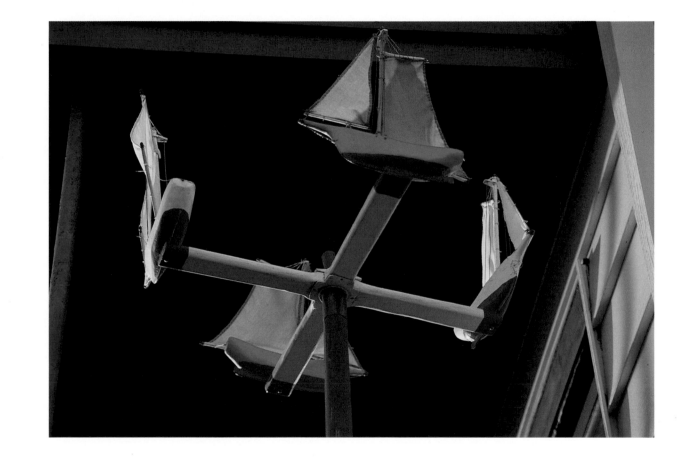

ROBERT ARSENAULT WILLIAM DUGAS ROBERT HICKS JOHN PINHORN
GEORGE AUGOT TERRANCE DWYER DEREK HOLDEN WILLIE POWELL
NICHOLAS BALDWIN DOMENIC DYKE ALBERT HOWELL GERALD POWER
KENNETH BLACKMORE DEREK ESCOTT ROBERT HOWELL DOUGLAS PUTT
THOMAS BLEVINS ANDREW EVOY ROBERT HOWLAND DONALD RATHBUN
DAVID BOUTCHER ROBERT FENEZ JACK JACOBSEN DENIS RYAN
WADE BRINSTON RANDELL FERGUSON CLIFF KUHL DARRYL REID
JOSEPH BURRY PETER FOGG HAROLD LEDREW RICK SHEPPARD
PAUL BURSEY RONALD FOLEY ROBERT LEDREW FRANK SMIT
GREG CAINES MELVIN FREID MICHAEL MAURICE WILLIAM SMITH (CAN)
KENNETH CHAFE CARL FRY RALPH MELENDY WILLIAM SMITH (U.S.A)
DAVID CHALMERS GEORGE GANDY ROBERT MADDEN TED STAPLETON
GERALD CLARKE GUY GARBEAU WAYNE MILLER KENT THOMPSON
DANIEL CONWAY REGINALD GORUM GORD MITCHELL GREG TILLER
GARY CRAWFORD CYRIL GREENE PERRY MORRISON CRAIG TILLEY
ARTHUR DAGG NORMAN HALLIDAY RANDY NOSEWORTHY GERALD VAUGHN
NORMAN DAWE FRED HARNUM KEN O'BRIEN WOODROW WARFORD
JIM DODD TOM HATFIELD PASCHAL O'NEILL MICHAEL WATKIN
THOMAS DONLON CLARENCE HAUSS GEORGE PALMER ROBERT WILSON
WAYNE DRAKE RON HEFFERNAN CLYDE PARSONS ROBERT WINSOR
LEON DRODDY GREGORY HICKEY DONALD PIEROWAY STEPHEN WINSOR

A plaque and monument to one of Newfoundland's more recent marine disasters. The semi-submersible drilling rig Ocean Ranger sank in a fierce winter storm in 1982, taking the entire crew of 84 with it.

The moon rising over Fort Amherst illuminates the harbour on a picture-perfect evening.

*As with gladness men of old
 Did the guiding star behold;
 As with joy they hailed its light,
 Leading onward, beaming bright.*
 —William Chatterton Dix